NOTHING FOR IT BUT TO SING

# NOTHING FOR IT
# BUT TO SING

poems

## MICHAEL HARLOW

OTAGO

Published by Otago University Press
Level 1, 398 Cumberland Street
Dunedin, New Zealand
university.press@otago.ac.nz
www.otago.ac.nz/press

First published 2016

ISBN 978-1-927322-62-8

Editor: Emma Neale
Design/layout: Fiona Moffat

Cover art by Catherine Day, based on an original sketch by the author

Printed in New Zealand by Printlink Ltd, Wellington

MICHAEL HARLOW is one of New Zealand's leading poets. He has published ten books of poetry including, most recently, *Sweeping the Courtyard: Selected poems* (2014), *Heart Absolutely I Can* (2014), *Cassandra's Daughter* (2005, 2006) and *The Tram Conductor's Blue Cap,* which was a finalist in the 2010 National Book Award for Poetry. His *Take a Risk, Trust Your Language, Make a Poem* was awarded the PEN/NZ Best First Book of Prose (1986). He has held the Katherine Mansfield Memorial Fellowship in Menton, France; the Randell Cottage Writer in Residence; and was the Burns Fellow (2009) and the inaugural Caselberg Artist in Residence (2009). He held the University of Otago Wallace Residency at the Pah Homestead (2011 –12); and was awarded the prestigious Lauris Edmond Memorial Award for Distinguished Contribution to New Zealand Poetry. He was the recipient of the NZSA Peter and Dianne Beatson Fellowship in 2015; that year *Nothing for it but to Sing* also won the Kathleen Grattan Award for an unpublished poetry manuscript.

# Contents

*To let words loose in their looking, and to hear*
*what it is that shines a light in the world's ear*


*When I think I'm dreaming of a horse, it turns out*
*to be a motorbike. And you know, I've never ridden*
*either. Still—I can dance and also skip*

—AUTHOR'S NOTEBOOKS


*One doesn't read poetry while thinking of other things.*

—GASTON BACHELARD

## 'Nothing for it but to sing'

*for Max*

You say your life is a narrow time in a black box.
That you are blanked. That there is only the one painting
before painting yourself out of the picture—heart's arrow
to the target, falling before it leaves the bow.

That all the blazoning voices of colour in you are stilled.
How to survive even yourself; a thought unwedded,
left there eating air. And then, an old song returning,
that you might seize the world with your hands.

Sometimes there is nothing for it but to sing; to discover
what there is in you to attain, when the light comes
stealing in: all the unlived in you that wants you.
The painting that says it is *the world that asks to be seen.*
Go there. Until the one painting becomes again a place to live.

## Short talk on spring with fantails

That far but always near place of feeling,
we called childhood. When we grew up
and discovered that it was still there
inside us, still the green song.
The way it has of returning us
to that someone we once were, and still
on the way to becoming someone we are.
And now that it's spring being sprung
all over, these friendly fantails air-dancing,
even daring to take bread at your hand.
To say there is something going on
that makes you want to take off and fly
across the green fields; that wakes in you
those wild-free times that keep turning
into music you get to play all over again.
And here in this little book of words,
you get to say other words that are sun-filled
enough to keep you turning corners
that once were straight lines—to meet
yourself again, and others just as wild-free
you haven't forgotten to remember: now
that spring has arrived, the first flowering
almond, makes you want to *risk delight*—
for its own sake and no other.

# Forgetting to remember

*To tell a love, one must write*

—Gaston Bachelard

If as Plotinus says memory
    is for those who have
forgotten, what is it that has
    so slipped your mind you
have forgotten how to remember
—the first and last time we
fell together; under such a blaze
    of stars, making all those
crazy wishes.

    By the time you stripped
down to your French underwear,
    worn you said for just this
special time, we had pledged each
    other those ever eternals—that
I see now make all the possibles
    impossible. We were looking
for the One thing we couldn't find
    a way of saying.

    That same night across town
your father who had been falling
    down all that year, finally did.
Your mother said the noise he made
    when he hit bottom, you can
on certain nights still hear. 'Losers
    take all' the note said—before

he put a bullet through his head.
    And my heart too, you said.


    And here now, to tell a love that
love always desires to say something
    about itself, one must write.
And remember a long night's vigil
    at the window. Waiting for someone
yourself to return with all those words
    we lost some longer years ago.

# The family at last

Oh, happy somebodies at last.
    Fluttering on their hooks,
such a family of clothes getting
    together again; and a little play
of expectations, a hat doffed,
    a sleeve or two shaking hands,
and waving 'Hello, I like the way
    you are looking today';
and a bodice full of steamy promises.

They are delighted to be lolling
about—eating air, leaning into
    each other, a little caress here
another there, and what looks like
    a discreet exchange of vows
from time to time. Hardly a wasp
    of a dark word between them.
'No need to hold on to who
    we once were'; happy now to be
emptied of their former lives—
    crossing frontier after frontier,
with no names to call their own.

# Short talk on hats

If hats can talk and tell as well as show, this story
    our family's treasured one by father favoured, returns
in all its winning ways. Oh, *mon chapeau,* his small shout
    of celebration. Streetwise, in all weathers of the year,
his old fedora for the common touch; and touch there
    was much of snappily to the brim. Such lifting and doffing.

This sharp slant or that neat tilt, the slight lift of recognition
    never failed to delight the eye; that touch of intimacy
that said more than any rush of syllables to the head.
    Spoke most warmly this gestural talk, when meeting
others on their daily parade—such a salute of heartfelt.
    Why, I do like the way you are looking today, if I may.

God bless and *sto kalo* and 'go with the good'. A good man
    he was, there's no bluff or vaunt in speaking so; his way
of saying more than the prettiness of pleasantries. More,
    I see now than any easy custom of hat-tricks convivial.
So small an act his talking hat, the flourishing goodness

of it feels true: to save some part of any day, losing itself
    to darkening times. The way heart-to-hand-to-hat,
the greater truth of himself, may re-story and return:
    that fellow feeling in brighter times, we used to call
by kindness, named.

## 'Not love's fault nor time's'

There is as much talk about and looking
out for time, as there is for love. How one
is always chasing down the other. Running
ahead or behind, turning into one thing
then another with astonishing ease.

Showing themselves in all their ways
in the book of happy and the book of sad.
Together so like the gods of nature, so beyond
prediction. And look: their dancing ways;
how they move in and out of each other.

How they lie down together, each time
inside the story that dares us to be more
than visitors on the way through. True,
there are those who talk of their cozening ways.
Still, something there is to be blazoned here.

Time and time again, I hear you say:
the true measure is all the heart's affection.
It's not love's fault it's not a miracle;
nor faulting time's lot, is it?

## Let's do it

She said I do and I will.
    And what's more, from the way
you are opening your heart
    to the deep of its feeling,

I think you will too.
    Then there's a pair of us.
Let's do it. Let's make touch
    and play, and the miracle

of words, be the way we arrange
    a story about the secret life
of all the green things that keep us
    so alive to each other.

Let there be no talk of paradise.
    Something there is in soul-making
that is more than the thrill
    of spending the rest of your life
being beautiful alone.

What we do in making earth
    and love that place to lie down
together—is enough to say,
    that for love there will always be
the music of light, opening
    the life of flowers, and ourselves.

## Reflections: in the wider world

*1*

We look to listen.
The eye so wedded
to the ear such intimacy,
always wanting to touch
each other. Such sensations.
How often they surprise
each other. And look—
you can hear how they
fall for each other, all over
again. Of course, they have
their own astonishments.
The world always the same
but different.


*2*

The oldest tree in the garden
of the world, keeping time,
and ours, to consider: how
this blazing almond is ever
directing the wind's music.
To say that spring is opening,
dressing up for earth's wedding
we are invited to, year after year ...

*3*
Listening
to what the silence
is trying to say.
All this noise.
I can hardly hear
the music of the water
running over stones,
how they rock and sing.

All this talk flying out
of heaven, swarms
of angels, wing-beat vibrato,
with so much to say
for themselves—the air
thick with them.

On arrival, they take names.
They take measurements,
from below to above.
The darting wing-tip
of a swallow passing by
catching the light of the eye.

It is also time to remember
that if you want to live long,
and love so—live old.

*4*

And out of the keepsake box,
his long affair with words,
dressed up for the occasion.
He had style. If you mean by that,
the secret life of the imagination
the curves of it, coming to light.
There are ways, he said, to survive
oneself and the world. All his life
he kept looking for the one song
to sing him. A high-wire troubador
on air, he said that writing
is the painting of the voice.
His wish that not one word be unsung.


*5*

This morning the colour of steel.
    And voices like skywriting
on air, the dark ripple of news
    that stills the day in its tracks.
The bird has lost its song; no more
    the Anatolian lark to wake to.
Everywhere, a dreadful quiet falls.
    The gold rings that have vanished;
no hands holding other hands;
    so many lovers gone crazy
in the heart.

6

*Eclipsed*

Stunned by the moon
losing its borrowed light
the growing dark—a voice
from inside the women's
prison floating down
from an open window,
What the fuck is
going on here, anyway?
she said. Who's that
turning out the lights?
Yesterday, I lost my name;
and today my kids too.
And now this—shaking
her fist, listen mister dark,
don't you dare.


7

Each night he tried to make a go of it.
    Love on its way out of town, trailing
astonishments; bells without sounds,
    inside them, no way he could
un-say all that he had said; to turn
    things around, to lie down again
to the deep call of her body.
    He couldn't possibly go back
on his words, could he?
    He didn't mean to say
what he meant to say, but did.

And for that, there is no rival
now in the house of sorrow:
   the fern owl's cry aloft, that
rakes the air, just before it strikes.


8

How this fossil-stone slips
into the palm of my hand,
still warm to the touch; its thumb-
print of sun, the script of years,
its weather-pitted face.
Buried there, the light-strike
of stars, sea-biscuit, the wizard-
shine of a Chinese moon on water.
Stroking its small pulse of life,
holding it up to the light,
this is amethyst—I can hear
there is music to be taken.


9

I'm always surprised
that people are helpful.
The wonder of it.

It had been snowing for days.
On the way to the clinic
for the old ones, I drove
into a lamp post. So many
people came running.
Talking with their hands.

And then an old man,
with a patch over one eye
put his hand through
the shattered window;
and rested it on my shoulder—
for what seemed a very short,
a very long time.

## 10
### *Curtain raiser*

The game, shadows
on the white wall of the church
of Saint Demetrios, our dazzling
recital stage—the play
of flashing hands, turning
into all the animals, parading
from the Ark; we are composing
names they have to live out,
we have to live up to.
To carry our secret thoughts,
we ask that: to see them
climb the air to tell us who
one day, we might become.

## 11

### Boustrophedon

Here you are inside the book
   of old words. How does it feel
to be written to be read, as a yoke
   of oxen ploughing ahead one way,
then turning back another?
   You could say you are having it
both ways. And all your days, losing
   one life, and gaining another.
How to survive even yourself.


## 12

### In that high place

That long swaying caravan
of dreams. In that high place,
where you can talk to the mountain
and it talks back in many voices.
Owl-eyed Athena on her knees,
throwing bones to wager
on which side of the next war
she will cast her charm of spells.
And strike a swifting hand
and hack her way through
cohorts on the other side.
It's never easy on some days,
to know who to betray
on other days, is it?

## Her words

She read the map of his hand.
Upturned the prophecy cup.
The easy sighs that were smiles.
Told him that water never talks
nonsense. The gypsy girl,
her singing bracelets; her eyes
fierce with the light of her riddling
words: that the early truth
of real love lives in the eye.
She said that all his dreams
were true. Even those not yet
borne on the wings of pretty birds.
And she kissed the air behind
his ear; and touched him there—
before he disappeared into that
great hole behind her words.

# The night-watch, making the rounds

Making the rounds was my job.
Tracking the hours, listening
to the hushed talk of time in the
small black box at my side.
Keeping an eye for any flicker
of shadow not my own.
A sharp ear for any heavy
breathing. Trying the locks.

Time and again, I heard
myself say no easy thing
to befriend the darkness.
When probing the dark-time
is the way you make my world
work. Even the mice in the walls
sleep safely when I'm about.

The comfort of doors that open
and close and never complain;
my shoes that never rise above
a whisper, I owe you the debt
of silent nights.

And these desks a little lonely
I think, such absences; such snowfalls
of paper waiting to be disturbed.
All these empty chairs waiting

for important ideas to return.
Hands to make everything happen.
Sometimes, I just want to sit down
and think it over; write a love note

to someone I'll never know.
Say something about the simple
beauty at morning light, of a single
fence post repeating itself, running

along a far-ridge—fence-dancing
on the horizon. And it's more than
just a pretty picture. Inside the dark
is the light. To know this—such a relief
from trying to understand too much.

# Aftershock

In the aftershock of a big one
    on the Richter, you came floating
by in your nightgown. And just over
    your shoulder the also-flying church

in search of the three bells calling out
    the fell end of your friendship
    with the things of the world. I thought
then of that time out of time when we

talked to the river and it talked back;
    and the clicking serenade of the
harvest cricket rising from the pale
    stubble. And the bright birds

and the dark birds shifting songs
    through the thicket of your heart.
When grandfather's cane was full
    of smiling conversations that ended

    with everyone shaking hands again.
And now, in the roiling heave of time
    you have been shaken down and turned
inside out. And you are closer to where god

shines a light in your ear. And you know,
    drawing the 'short straw', you are finally
going to have a crack at the silky darkness.

## 'Not in our stars'

Confusing the dark of the world
its heavy breathing with the light
astonishments of its laughter—
he has made a holy mess of it.

Keeps wanting to be the only story
in town. To play a starring role in love
with everyone, and himself; talking non-
stop so ardently to the empty chair

in the corner of his room. He is waiting
for the one to return, who has not
forgotten that when you catch a bird,
sing to it, then let it go. The one

who has words for who has gone missing.
How then to make the world called
himself come right? And here he is—
looking deep into the mirror, to see

what might be behind it all. And all
that he can see—himself, and no other,
standing perfectly in his own way.

## No full stops in heaven

In no hurry, you play the game of overstay.
    Insomnia's pal you are everywhere
the good sleep is not. You get around
    like the dark itself, always waiting

to make the right call. Only a visitor,
    you say? Such a swarm of nightlong
whispers, you mug the ear; and you crave
    such wakefulness, all the hours of all

the time left in the world. A siren song.
    The gods of sleep have lost their way
you say, no embraces more. Looking
    over your shoulder, I can see

even the art of dying is somehow
    something we haven't to deserve.
Something about being condemned
    to live with who we are.

And you are sure, having made the return
    trip again and again: there are no
full stops in heaven, to look homeward to.

## The late news

This little boy
with his new number-one
haircut, his heart full of surprise,
clutching his end-of-the-year report card
to his chest, crossing High Street
for the last time—without looking
both ways

His black and white dog,
her snappy tail on fast forward
waiting for him, ears pricked,
on the other side, the cars
streaming by

Mother at the upstairs
open window, ironing
the family clothes, humming
a familiar tune for company,
just before raising her head
to look down into the street
of the dead

Later, on the late news
someone, a bystander looking
for some lost words—that kid
he said. Not a chance.
You know today is the longest
day of the year, and it's
going to last forever

# Post mortem on promises

Not long after they met at one of the bookstalls
   along the Seine, this one draped with streamers
of sheet music, she promised that she would always
   dream of them together, naturally, in French.

*She loves me, she loves me not, she loves me not,*
   *she loves me* … Such promises he told himself
are promises of the heart. And they live there,
   and are more than the play of noughts

and crosses. And then the day you discover
   a wreath of broken flowers at your feet.
The fallen petals a still life, *nature morte*.
   The first time she left and the last, he splashed

a circle of water behind her, calling out, 'May it
   not dry before you return.' There are times
you don't know which life to trust, even your own.

## Cage-masters, their want

The cages are waiting.
For centuries they have been waiting.
Even before they have been hammered
and welded together, waiting to be stroked.
Even before, they are hoisted into the air;
and hooded to imprison the light,
everywhere, along the leafy boulevards.
And the cage-masters? Always,
they embrace their want to cage a song.
There are decisions to be worried.
Measurements to be taken;
not too small, not too spacious;
these master cages. And they say,
yes—there is the one size;
the tomb-size of a child; of a fledgling
learning its music. They say, snapping
their fingers to each other: yes, the size
of a bird—the one in search of a cage.

# Hidden hurts

They add up. They do their bruising work
    on the sly. All those hidden hurts
of everyday life. How they rely on sleight-
    of-word a swarm of whispers that stun

the ear. They hit the heart when you're
    looking the other way. You can spend
forever trying to hear what it is you haven't
    heard for fear it might drop you to your knees.

This uncle, years of cutting hair and trading
    talk as small as he could make it. Each
shave a little closer; and bringing home
    the money that bought smiles at table.

And here he is, shaking down the bedclothes
    for bad dreams; turning his sleeves
inside out to take hold of something that
    isn't there. Watching the pendulum clock

in the darkened parlour, telling itself
    the time in the house that no one
has lived in for years. You know, he said,
    my mother died before she was born;

and that was years before my time.
    This uncle who kept talking the life
out of himself. One cut of scissors, then
    another like this, and another, like this.

# Beyond

Quite by co-incident, I'd like to think it that,
I met my twin, dead brother—on the leafy green
corner of the town park, where we used to watch
as kids the flying nuns in their starched habits, sailing

out early mornings on the playground swings;
and higher than we dared to imagine—the thrill
of it, their glancing laughter. And here, my brother
as if arriving himself under sail, on the wings

of a waking dream; a man still young as he was old.
And that desperate curiosity of his that kept him
chasing the untold story of his life; the one
about, who's missing? Our governess, kissing

us off to sleep. The rocking horse in the nursery
that he is still riding. Before we could say hello again
and goodbye, looking me straight in the eye,
and beyond—he said, not a song to sing

for my supper. The gods need more than
that, don't they? What it was he saw 'beyond'
where his looking had gone, there's no telling.

Something he once said, that cast such a shadow
on his returning, sailing on out of sight:
the dead are always shuffling behind, sure
to catch up, when the time is right.

# Then there's a pair of us

When they found him in the middle
of the empty field—one shoe on
the other off, holding it aloft
a salute to something unseen

but there. Shouting out to the dark,
'I didn't do it, did you?' And they
asked him what he was looking for
out there alone with himself, under

the brushwork of stars, small islands
of fallen light. He was he said staking
a claim. About losing something,
so that one day he might find it again.
If the gods relent. I'm looking for nothing
you could put a name to right now.
Of course, it's hard work, and my head
hurts. You see, I'm nobody to speak of.

You know, for nobody, nothing
is sincerely difficult to find; and now
that you have arrived: are you nobody too?

# When no birds sang

When he fell out of the world's work,
into no arms to hold him—or stay
the crazed confusion of his time, he
felt himself getting smaller than small.

Until there was no one there at all.
'It's like the iron entering my heart,'
he said. And there is nowhere else
to go. It was then, he fell into the dark

hole of days. Such hours. The stopped
clock. Something about the heart knows
more than understanding can say.

Not being wanted anywhere to do
your share, makes nowhere the terror.
Instinct with elegy, he feared that when
he hit bottom there would be no sound

to follow after. And he stayed there.
Until one morning when no birds sang,
emptied of all that can be said,
soul-window open—he woke up dead.

# Bite the bright coin its brilliance

*The 'Grabbers', they are everywhere*
*such a dark swarm; and they clone*
*themselves, that's more than a worry.*
*Instinct with egomania, that's more*
*than a name . . .*

1  They say you may be truly gifted, the good
fortune that you yourself have made. Your hands
are everywhere that capture the purse. You say
there is a decency that winner takes all, and all
there is to be taken. You trust your reach for the
'good as gold'. And you bite the bright coin its
brilliance

2  Take hold, then, and pleasure yourself. And a
delighting kiss in the mirror as silky as the
moon's touch. Keep spies to tell you everything.
Have ears everywhere

3  Blazoning headlines be star-bright to dazzle the
public eye. Be crowned the emperor of the Midas
horde

4  Here's how to pilfer and filch, and be rewarded.
Stash the all of it in your best bank. Then put the
bank in a box. Carefully, put the box in the dark of
your pocket. On the way out a bravura flourish
turn all the locks to silly to such helplessness as
will confound the world. And slip away as

stealthily as you entered the richness of your time.
Wear a bowler hat for safety

5 Homeward bound, a scampering pleasure that in
you swells. To the cars in their stalls buffed to a
sheen. To the dear wife who is reading a book
about how and how often. Already she is stripping
down to her birthday. You might think that heaven
is no further away than a 'quick one'. To the kids
who have been caressed to sleep by nanny. Who is
quite a number herself

6 And now as you open the door, slip through, a
shine in your eye, with flowers for
the dearness in them. With a fat sigh that has your
name all over it, call it a day richly spent. And a
life too.

# Hidden things

*after Cavafy*

It was no more a shouting honour
to be gloried by the statue he had become.
Takings were small. Trifles fit for lesser gods.

And those dressed in their sorrows,
who came to whisper pleads under cover
of the dark, he could no longer
make any thought sing to be wise in reply.

Even when the finest Parthian marble
and lurid daubs of colour played into the hands
of young girls, who dared to come calling;
their fondling questions, their dreams

steaming with more than household prettiness.
In return, his small noises of broken words.
Once dedicated to Hermes the wily one,
he couldn't count on what might happen next.

And then it did. So many years waiting
for the barbarians to arrive. The flight
of rumour, running the streets with stories
of their dark enlightenment. And here he is,

hauled to the city gates. Their horses steaming
with sweat; the clamour of their weapons
beaten bronze. The bolder ones in the crowd,
crowing, 'good wreaths', fisting the air,

the thrill of such words promising the world.
Trusting in his dreams that they are the keepers
of *hidden things*—he is waiting to be taken.

## Eating the silence

Struck by the quick fall of dark across
her shoulders, like a bruised hurt
returned to deepen itself, she felt it
entering her body to stay. And she sat
there—in the cane chair that hadn't gone
anywhere in years. Wish after walkabout
wish, slipping away. Until she was emptied
of all those words that might have made
a difference. Eating the silence night
after night. There are so many ways
to leave the world, she said, looking hard
at her hands, that kept losing their way.
Thinking of those eighteen floors
to the paving stones; the long fall
into nowhere at all—and all a vanished
time. And she is waiting now, for those
fleet falls of shadow to begin their
nightly pitch along the deep street.

# Above and below

On the lookout against that time
    when our tongues will be taken away
in boxes. Be swivel-eyed. Be quick

    to sniff the air, like the shrew-mole
in the crackling stubble. The ones,
    who would have us out of hiding

to please our darker selves come stalking.
    To please some thought, why it is
we need these furious enemies, ours.

Who come from no further away,
    than ourselves we are. Who enter
by the front door cradling armfuls

of yellow flowers, and leave by the back,
    strewing blood-red anemones that
wind-wild, fly. Some fiercer truth there is

that says, 'There is so much out there
    in the open, so many constellations
of desire; and below, there is what

is hidden in ourselves. It is what is hidden,
    the light in the darkness, that is the
real world—the one we have been
    dreaming about, for longer lives
than we have forgotten to remember.'

## The discovery of morning

Discovering the morning is more
than just a wake up and hello,
are you still there? It was the year
one of our parents kept disappearing
to somewhere and then returning.

And this particular morning, the yellow
noise of the birds; the colour of my sister's
hair drying in the sunlight, and shining
fiercely. The colour of the lion's mane
in the story that used to prowl up and
down at the door of our sleeping room.

It was my sister who always wanted
to be the lion-tamer. She wore a lion-tamer's
moustache, and rolled up her sleeves
to show the small bulge of her muscles.
And she was quick with the cut of her words,
and a small whip of willow twigs.
For years love seemed so far away
and gone—before I cared to like her again.

## Arriving at Delphi

To riddle not
for the unfathomable,
but to find some words
for the unnameable.

To know why today
the dead are always
behind us in a hurry
to start a conversation.

And how it is tomorrow
we may fall back in love
out of those small hatreds
that racked the heart hard.

To hear again the world song
of astonishing laughter.
In the palm of your hand,
this flying dolphin, the finest

Cycladic marble; in your pocket
seven white mice for Apollo.
And the dream of arriving
at Delphi to hear the news.
And these marble statues—
what songs do they sing
here, to wake up to?

# Take five: composition for words and music

Throw *Time* a spanner, against
prediction too.
Make this rehearsal each moment
a first performance.

Play what you hear *furioso,*
an explosive
occasion of celebration; then a little
*dolcissimo*

from the heart. Take five: to consider
the loud blur
of hands coming together. Or the deep
silence that arrives

there first. Do not think about *virtuoso,*
no, star attractions.
They are such a distraction.
Now, repeat

all green-coloured notes for 4′33″:
Listen, for who is
master and servant here. Your songs say
no one is leading

anyone more than they need to.
Let these words
be 'daughter to the music'. Take five:
then begin again

*appassionato.* 'You can hear,' he says,
'there is no love without music.'
Play, what you hear: let all words
be the music of song.

# This is your birthday

He had always wanted to end up
as a constellation in the night sky.
Sending out all that starlight to cover
the earth. To leave behind a map

of himself. Better the dream to make
true than the nightmare to play false,
he thought, on waking to a green time.
And he worried that if he failed

to love greatly, he would fall early
out of himself. And her words now,
hurrying from one empty room
to another. She says on leaving
you know, the heart never lies more
than it needs to. Look, behind you—
this is your birthday. And you are
always ten years old.

# Inventory

The coin of light that fell
into the palm of his hand.
The quick surprise of it,
and the flung star travelling

all time to find him at home.
Telling his beads. In the small
white-washed room, learning
to be alone with himself; trying

to notice things for the first time.
In the map of his hand, the years:
all those stories waiting for what
secret wish that sits in the middle

and knows. On the blue table
the ace of hearts his calling card.
And then from a far time the more
near, the cry of the night owl—its
strangeness at the heart of the familiar.

# The invitation

Learning how to live inside
the darkness that owned her.
Waking from a thrashing sleep,
she slipped out into the still street;
to listen to the dreaming conversations
of the neighbourhood. To rescue herself
from the black horse of her dreams
that wanted to ride her. Its wings
folding and unfolding, an invitation.

Like the dog on its leash, her white stick
searching the dark. At the end of the street,
the intense quiet of the blacksmith's shop.
Not even a hurried hand of wind
ruffling the stillness. The undressed silence.
Listening. Nearby, the shivery call
of the black horse—waiting to be mounted.

# The holiness of attention

With the open palm of his left hand,
he beat the child's drum found under
the olive trees—left there by one of the
guards, with his sweat-stained cap.

All the long summer, the feverish chatter
of the cicadas. Already, the late light
falling into the bodies of trees still standing
freely on their own. The young teacher,

who had arrived during the night,
opened his mouth but said nothing—
his words snatched away by the rasping
swipe of the wind sweeping across

the courtyard. Waiting for their names
to be called. Body count the dark game.
The older ones, turning their backs to the sea.
Waiting for their numbers to be shouted out.

With the fist of his right hand, striking
the drum again and again, until
the severe quiet returned. The youngest
one, pressing his face against the wall,

afraid to call out. Like the others, waiting
for some words to leap up. For the child
he once was to be here; walking across the swing
bridge, holding a key of shining yellow

in his hand. To take the imagination into the heart;
before the darkness blanked his eyes. Waiting
for the barking fox on the hill to be heard.
This is called at last, the holiness of attention.

# Matrimonial, on a train

The twin nuns.
Their impeccably groomed and starched habits,
almost a wonder; such a quiet music between them.
Sharing a single seat on the train, on their way
to a retreat, the elected silence of their desire.
Holding hands against the cradle-rocking
of the carriage. Their shining elation,
such unshadowed pleasure, brides of Christ.
As the train began its upward, swaying climb
into the mountains, the confetti of snow flurries
at the window, their gold rings kissing
each other, lightly.

# A deeper call

Gone now.
All his lights out.
Our town crazy who loved fires
and chased them; on his bad days
they chased him back he said,
pumping like mad his beauty
*Schwinn* in fire-truck red,
his bike-bell drilling the air.
Taking on that fiery shadow,
I'd like to think on our behalf;
enough to hold him dearly.
I can still hear him and now,
a striking music to the ear;
he is shouting over and again,
keeping time to a deeper call,
'My name is Elsinore, or else—'

## Miss Jones in Haberdashery

Widowed young, now old alone.
    Miss Jones with a striking head of hair.
With glancing smiles, we imagined song-birds
    nesting there. She had a thing about hats,
Miss Jones. Some kind of desire unspoken,
    we thought, that made her smile a little sad.
It was said she could sell even what wasn't
    there, but one dreamy day would be.
She knew more than just the price, Miss Jones.

    In any heave of wind, if you should see
a headless hat out and about, tumbling
    down the street, gusting left then right,
in a sudden darting ploy, cross to the other
    side, and against the light—just reach out,
and lift it into the air, and wear it: all the wind-driven
    way home, as you imagine Miss Jones, her small
smile, who knows more than just the price.

## Last post

One of the men leaning on his shovel;
talking to the other one, his look-alike,
leaning on the same shovel, listening:

'This war will soon be ended,' he said.
And he spit into the narrow trench
they were trying to make come true.

'Yes,' he said, 'until the next one arrives;
the children will pour from our houses,
their fists in their eyes.' Overhead,
flocks of birds casting shadows

over the earth. Staring into each other's
eyes for a long moment—they could see,
that there was no one looking back.
And their children, waiting for years
in their darkened rooms, for the all-clear.

# The company of mapmakers

In the company of mapmakers you are one.
     When you lay out the world there are no
straight lines. There is only clamouring for it
     in occluded offices where high words plump
for the 'straight and narrow', and are bluster.

The only rule that's truly to itself is clear:
     turn, and *follow the stories*. And the stories inside
them is what mapmakers do. They are never
     in a hurry to discover, how the mind's thought

feels its way through the dark, and the light
     of the dark. To see what it feels like to follow
earth's curve, the shape of what you imagine,
     and are imagined by. An art to make surprise

a wonder. There is so much that turns into
     laughter buried here—to follow the song
of hurrying water; to recall the 'river of rivers',
     rushing to the sea to lose its name, then

returning to take another. In word-struck
     lines of optic infatuation you are mapping
the territory to make the invisible, visible.
To know how the impossible is possible,

when it is like this: 'the air is full of flying
     children'; trees so musical they are scoring
     harmonies of a heaven. And to know

the fine turbulence of women, and then,
    their quietude. To find a place to be.

Mapmakers never play false; and they know,
    how not knowing is on the way to arriving.
When they say, there is no one thing naturally
    alone, on either side of the great divide.

That today's map is tomorrow the same,
    but always different. Losing your way,
as you will, the mapmakers' lyric, is also
    the way of finding it, and yourself, again.

# The piano's birthday

*for Eira Stenberg*

Today I saw the star
I fell from
a blaze of light
felt it enter my body.

Like the green song
of the earth—the Marjatta
tree its blood-red
bursting forth

In the still, noon-tide
quiet of the Plaza Colón,
the silvery notes of a piano
being played in an empty room

We hear: the music
of years; and the lost voices
of the sun returning:
from this the poem springs.

# Notes

**Forgetting to remember**: 'To tell a love, one must write', by French philosopher and poet Gaston Bachelard: *The Poetics of Reverie: Childhood, language, and the cosmos* (Boston: Beacon Press, 1969, 2004). 'Memory is for those who have forgotten': these words come from the Neoplatonist Plotinus, as quoted by Eliot Weinberger in 'Memory Karma Smell' (*Sulfur 36,* 1995).

**Short talk on spring with fantails** and **Short talk on hats**: Acknowledgment to poet, translator and classical scholar Anne Carson for this as a title inscription. See *Short Talks*, Anne Carson (London, Ontario: Brick Books, 2005).

**Reflections: in the wider world**: The phrase 'if you want to live long, / and love so—live old', is from a literary postcard, which attributes the words to the French composer Erik Satie: *Si vous voulez vivre longtemps, vivez vieux*. In section 11, *Boustrophedon*: an ancient method of writing in which the lines run alternately from right to left and from left to right, in the manner of oxen ploughing.

**Then there's a pair of us**: The words *'are you nobody too?'* refer to Emily Dickinson's poem, 'If I'm nobody, are you nobody too?': number 42 in *The Selected Poems of Emily Dickinson*, edited by James Reeves (London: Heinemann, 1963).

**When no birds sang**: The phrase 'soul-window open': in many parts of Europe it was customary to have in the bedroom/sleeping-room a small window as a section of the larger one, which could be opened at the time of death, so that the soul could ascend to heaven. In this poem I am thinking of such a 'soul-window' in a *baurenhaus* in the small village Zwillikon, just over an alpine pass near Zürich.

**Hidden things**: The title is from the Alexandrian Greek poet Kavafy (Cavafy) and his poem of the same title. See C.P. Cavafy, *Passions and Ancient Days,* selected and translated by Edmond Keeley and George Savvides (New York: New Dial, 1971). My poem is an instance of a poem being imagined forward in time. 'Hermes the wily one': the Greek god Hermes (the Roman Mercury), had many attributes and exploits. He could invent the lyre one morning and later the same day steal the cattle of his brother, Apollo. Hermes is also known as *psychopómpos* (a conductor of souls to the underworld) and the trickster god: adroit, cunning, mischievous and magical.

**Arriving at Delphi**: A sanctuary sacred to Apollo as the god of light (he has many other attributes). I am thinking of the 'light of consciousness'.

**Take five: composition for words and music:** the numerical reference 4′33″ is to John Cage's avant-garde and highly influential piano work, performed by David Tudor. The only sounds heard were that of 'silence', and the sounds around that silence.

**The company of mapmakers:** The phrase 'the air is full of flying children' is from 'Chaos in Motion and not in Motion', Wallace Stevens, *The Collected Poems* (1954), (New York: Vintage/Random House, 1990).

**The piano's birthday:** 'Today I saw the star/I fell from': acknowledgement to the eleven-year-old poet Feng, who at the time of this poem's composition lived and wrote in Broad Bay on the Otago Peninsula, Dunedin, NZ.

# Acknowledgements

Grateful acknowledgement is made to the editors of the magazines and anthologies in which some of these poems first appeared: *Bravado*, *brief 41*, *broadsheet /14*, *Landfall*, *Metro*, *Otago Daily Times*, *Prime* (a folio of hand-printed poems by master printer Caren Florance (Otakou Press), *Takahe*, *Confabulario*, *Segunda Epoca* (Mexico), *Anthologia*, *Poezia Universale de Astazi* (Romania), *Revista de Prometeo* (Colombia), Marco Nerero Rotelli, *Poesia e Luce*, Venezia 2015 (art installation, 'Poetry and Light', Venice 2015).

I would like to thank the University of Otago, the Department of English and Linguistics and the Caselberg Trust for their generous support during my tenure as the Robert Burns Fellow in 2009. Special thanks to Otago University Press, publisher Rachel Scott, and to the Kathleen Grattan Award, which made possible the publication of *Nothing for it but to Sing*. And thanks to Emma Neale for her editorial acumen, and her deep understanding of how poetry does what it does.

# Also by Michael Harlow

### Poetry
*Edges*, 1974
*Nothing but Switzerland and Lemonade*, 1980
*Today is the Piano's Birthday*, 1981
*Vlaminck's Tie*, 1985
*Giotto's Elephant*, 1991
*Cassandra's Daughter*, 2005, 2006
*The Tram Conductor's Blue Cap*, 2009
*Sweeping the Courtyard: Selected poems*, 2014
*Heart Absolutely I Can*, 2014

### Prose
*Take a Risk, Trust Your Language, Make a Poem*, 1986
*Heavy Traffic in the Dark: Film script with Stephanie Donald*, 1991
*Poetry and Psychoanalysis: The place of the imagination, the imagination of place* (first published in Spanish as *Poesía y Psycoanálisis: Lugar de Imaginacion, Imagicion del Lugar*), 2006

### Texts/libretti: with composer Kit Powell
*Stone Poem*, 1976
*Devotion to the Small*, 1980
*Texts for Composition*, 1981
*Poem Then, for Love*, 1983
*Nelson Songs*, 1986
*Stations of the Clock*, 1986
*Les Épisodes: Conversation with questions*, 1987
*Father's Telescope*, 1989
*The Green Man*, 1989
*Today is the Piano's Birthday*, 2005
*The Tower of Babel*, 2006
*Missa Profana/Missa Natura*, 2010
*Microzoic Piano Suite*, 2012
*Symphonie Réflectique*, 2016

### Edited
*Events, Greece 1967–74*
*The Caxton Press Poetry Series*